Narmin Rajabova

Politics of the South Caucasus countries at the present stage

Narmin Rajabova

Politics of the South Caucasus countries at the present stage

ScienciaScripts

Imprint
Any brand names and product names mentioned in this book are subject to trademark, brand or patent protection and are trademarks or registered trademarks of their respective holders. The use of brand names, product names, common names, trade names, product descriptions etc. even without a particular marking in this work is in no way to be construed to mean that such names may be regarded as unrestricted in respect of trademark and brand protection legislation and could thus be used by anyone.

Cover image: www.ingimage.com

This book is a translation from the original published under ISBN 978-620-2-05269-6.

Publisher:
Sciencia Scripts
is a trademark of
Dodo Books Indian Ocean Ltd. and OmniScriptum S.R.L publishing group

120 High Road, East Finchley, London, N2 9ED, United Kingdom
Str. Armeneasca 28/1, office 1, Chisinau MD-2012, Republic of Moldova, Europe
Printed at: see last page
ISBN: 978-620-7-69784-7

Table of contents

Chapter 1: Security in the Caucasus at the present stage

Today, a vacuum of security and sustainable development at the regional level has emerged in the South Caucasus region. In fact, the countries of the South Caucasus region live in a state of constant and sustainable military and political instability, which is fraught with a rapid escalation of conflict.

The geopolitical situation in and around the South Caucasus is changing so dynamically that it gives grounds to make the following intermediate conclusions: **first, the** priorities of US and NATO foreign policy in the South Caucasus have changed significantly. **Secondly, the** Russian Federation (RF) and the Islamic Republic of Iran (IRI), on the one hand, competing, and on the other hand, cooperating with each other, are trying to occupy the vacuum created in the region. And what is happening in the region is a de facto attempt to create a condominium between the Russian Federation and the IRI in the South Caucasus, which may lead to a decrease in the political sovereignty of Armenia, Azerbaijan and Georgia. When two strong regional players come to a consensus, they have a strong impact on the countries of the region, which is what is happening in the South Caucasus. And this puts the countries of the South Caucasus region in a vulnerable position and only improves the geostrategic and geo-economic position of the Russian Federation and the IRI.

Therefore, it can be stated that in the medium term the main line of geopolitical confrontation between the US-EU-NATO and Russia passes through the South Caucasus, Ukraine and Moldova, and the outcome of the above-mentioned "soft confrontation" depends, **firstly, the** vector of long-term geopolitical development of Armenia, Azerbaijan, Georgia, Moldova and Ukraine, **secondly, the** resolution of interethnic conflicts in Moldova and the South Caucasus region, and **thirdly, the** preservation or loss of political sovereignty of the above-mentioned states.

Today, it can be stated that the Russian Federation and the Islamic Republic of Iran have an identical position on the Karabakh issue: the status quo cannot and should not be changed due to Azerbaijan's military victory over Armenia. Consequently, official Baku and official Yerevan in the short term are forced to continue the search for peaceful means to settle Armenian-Azerbaijani relations through the prism of Russian and Iranian interests.

The Kremlin keeps under its control the internal political situation and foreign policy of official Yerevan, as well as manipulates the aspirations of official Tbilisi to establish relations with the Russian Federation and peacefully resolve inter-ethnic conflicts in Georgia (the South Ossetian and Abkhaz conflicts).

The Russian Federation demonstrates to both the West and the countries of the South Caucasus its intention to maintain the status quo in the balance of power between Azerbaijan and Armenia. Thus, official Moscow, on the one hand, sells some types of offensive weapons and military equipment to Azerbaijan, which increases the military potential of official Baku, but, on the other hand, the Kremlin has multiplied its military-technical assistance to Armenia and is strengthening its 102nd military base in Gyumri. After all, it is the Kremlin that acts as the de jure and de facto guarantor of Armenia's and Nagorno-Karabakh's security. It is logical that Armenia favors strengthening the CSTO structures.

Official Moscow seeks to create a through railroad from Russia to Armenia, which would greatly strengthen the Kremlin's military and political presence in the South Caucasus region, including on the Armenian-Turkish border. However, official Tbilisi, despite the voiced initiatives of Georgian ex-minister Paata Zakareishvili, is pragmatically in no hurry to actually participate in the implementation of the Russian project.

The fact is that the Abkhazian section of the Georgian railroad is privatized by Russian Railways (RZD). And if Georgia agrees to extraterritoriality of the Abkhazian section, it will de facto recognize the independence of Abkhazia, which is not in the plans of the Georgian government.

In turn, official Tbilisi intends to actively promote the peaceful process of resolving the Georgian-Abkhaz and Georgian-South Ossetian conflicts. In particular, the Georgian Government is abandoning Mikheil Saakashvili's previous position that the Georgian-Abkhazian and Georgian-South Ossetian conflicts are not independent processes but merely derivative elements of the Georgian-Russian confrontation.

By the way, legalization of identity documents issued in Abkhazia and South Ossetia made it possible not only for holders of such documents to move freely throughout the territory of Georgia, but also for them to receive medical care, education and so on.

Domestic political developments in Georgia after the parliamentary elections of 2012 and the presidential elections of 2013 and 2017 have had a favorable impact on the Kremlin's foreign policy in the South Caucasus region. Although, Georgia is not going to curtail its relations with the U.S. and NATO. At the same time, official Tbilisi has softened its foreign policy towards Russia, which negatively affects the Euro-Atlantic integration of both Georgia, Azerbaijan and Armenia.

The UK and France are actually represented in Azerbaijan rather than the EU. In particular, British Petroleum ("BP") and French "Total" are operators in the already implemented oil and gas projects in the AR ("Baku-Tbilisi-Ceyhan", "Baku-Tbilisi-Erzurum", "Azeri-Chirag-Guneshli" and "Shah Deniz") and are considered potential participants in the planned energy transportation projects in Azerbaijan (Absheron block and TANAP gas pipeline). Thus, reports of the US Department of Energy suggest that proven oil reserves in AR are more than 7 billion barrels and proven natural gas reserves are 849.5 billion cubic meters. In addition, additional gas reserves were discovered in 2011 at the offshore fields Umid and Absheron.

It is logical that British and French companies, i.e. Great Britain and France, wish to provide the TANAP project with blue fuel from the 2nd stage of the Shah Deniz gas fields on the Azerbaijani shelf in the Caspian Sea, which will allow them to participate directly in the realization of the TANAP project with all the ensuing consequences in the issue of the EU energy security growth.

It can be stated that official London and official Paris are interested, on the one hand, in reducing Russian gas supplies and, on the other hand, in preserving the existing status quo in the South Caucasus region, including with regard to conflict resolution (Karabakh, Abkhazia and South Ossetia).

Some circles in Paris and London believe that an evolutionary change in the status quo in the South Caucasus region is impossible to achieve, as the Kremlin is not going to give up its geopolitical and geostrategic priorities in favor of the realization of geo-economic interests of the above-mentioned European countries. And that is why France and Great Britain for the above-mentioned reasons seek to prevent the resumption of hostilities in the Karabakh conflict zone. After all, official Yerevan has repeatedly stated that in case of resumption of hostilities on the part of official Baku, Armenia will disable Azerbaijan's oil and gas infrastructure.

But, in reality, the Kremlin, arming Azerbaijan, will not allow official Baku to solve the Karabakh conflict in its favor by force of modern weapons and military equipment, i.e. to defeat CSTO member Armenia, and most importantly - official Moscow has actually received a real opportunity to control all energy transport projects of Azerbaijan in the South Caucasus, including TANAP.

The Kremlin does not want to give Azerbaijan the opportunity to organize large supplies of Azerbaijani gas to Europe, as the Russian "Turkish Stream" should implement this mission in the southern direction, especially official Moscow will not allow the supply of Turkmen natural gas to Europe.

It can be assumed that the Kremlin, pushing official Baku towards the "Karabakh blitzkrieg", hopes to solve three strategic tasks, which together can lead to Azerbaijan's defeat: **first, to** prevent Azerbaijani natural gas supplies to Europe; **second, to** make it impossible to implement the TANAP project, which will prevent Turkmenistan from supplying its natural gas to the EU countries; **third, to** take control of the financial flows of Azerbaijan and Turkmenistan with all the ensuing negative consequences for the economies of both countries.

The Kremlin has clearly demonstrated by the example of Armenia that official Moscow intends to implement its geopolitical project in the post-Soviet space with the participation of the majority of post-Soviet republics, including the participants of the Eastern Partnership program, with all the ensuing negative consequences for Armenia, Azerbaijan, Ukraine and Moldova, as well as the U.S., EU and NATO in their quest for strategic assertion in the Black Sea-Caucasus-Caspian region.

It can be argued that Armenia's accession to the Eurasian Economic Union (EAEU) has changed the balance of power in the South Caucasus region, including along the "Baku-Moscow" and "Baku-Yerevan" lines.

Armenia's de facto loss of its political and economic sovereignty in foreign policy has significantly increased the Kremlin's opportunities in the South Caucasus region, including the political settlement of the Karabakh conflict.

On the one hand, there is currently no activation of the OSCE MG against the background of the Kremlin-inspired "failure" of the Russian initiative to resolve the Karabakh conflict within the trilateral format of the Presidents of Azerbaijan, Armenia and Russia. It is logical that after repeated meetings of the Presidents of Azerbaijan, Armenia and Russia, official Baku and official Yerevan have further distanced themselves from the search for compromise solutions in the process of peaceful settlement of the Karabakh conflict under the auspices of the OSCE Minsk Group, as the Russian format of conflict resolution leads to the loss of sovereignty of the two South Caucasus countries.

It can be stated that the Kremlin has no real military-political and economic leverage over official Baku. Moreover, Ukraine, Georgia and Moldova, with the support of the EU, the US and NATO, are able to withstand Russian pressure, which will allow official Baku to preserve its political sovereignty.

Chapter 2: Turkey's Strategic Goals in the South Caucasus 2010-2015.

The foreign policy doctrine of official Ankara with regard to trilateral formats of cooperation between Turkey and the Republic of Azerbaijan (AR) and Georgia in the South Caucasus region, as well as between Turkey and AR and Turkmenistan in the Caspian region is realized within the framework of the concept of "strategic depth", the main idea of which is, among other things, the growth of Turkish influence in the Black Sea-Caucasus-Central Asia region and the transformation of the country into a regional "superpower". By the way, the regional policy of official Ankara in the Black Sea-Caucasus-Central Asian region is closely integrated with official Baku within the framework of realization of the slogan "one nation - two states".

In addition, official Ankara is an important trade partner for AR (imports from Turkey account for more than 11% - this is the 2nd place after the Russian Federation). Energy cooperation between AR and Turkey is realized through well-known energy transportation projects. Another important partner of Turkey in the South Caucasus is Georgia. Thus, for Georgia, both in export (more than 17 %) and import (more than 15 %) operations Turkey is in the first place.

Official Ankara's foreign policy towards the Republic of Azerbaijan (AR) is inextricably linked to Turkey's foreign policy concept towards the South Caucasus region.

In particular, Turkey, against the background of the freezing of Turkish-European relations, seeks, firstly, to take control of the "Southern Energy Transport Corridor" with all the ensuing consequences for both the EU and official Ankara, and secondly, intends to approve in the AR the concept of building a country on the basis of Islamic values, while preserving the pan-Turkic ideology and the foreign policy course of official Baku for further integration of the country within the framework of the Turkish geopolitical project. It can be argued that Turkey is interested in the Turkic world acquiring an organizational structure that will allow it to act in a coordinated and effective manner.

But most importantly, official Ankara wants to consolidate all Turkic states under the aegis of Turkey, which will lead to the creation of a single political and economic union of Turkic states. It should be noted that the above geopolitical project is generally supported by the U.S. and the EU, which are interested in limiting Russian and Chinese influence in the South Caucasus and Central Asia (CA) region. In turn, for the Russian Federation (RF), the Turkish geopolitical project is a threat in the context of the realization of the Eurasian Economic Union.

It is natural that AR and Turkey signed the "Treaty on Strategic Partnership and Mutual Assistance" on August 16, 2010.

It is symbolic that the above-mentioned agreement was concluded between the AR and Turkey a few days before the visit of Russian President Dmitry Medvedev to the Republic of Armenia (RA), within the framework of which agreements in the military-political and military-technical spheres were concluded between the RF and RA.

In other words, there are two de jure and de facto configurations of the regional security system in the South Caucasus: AR-Turkey (NATO member) and RA-RF (both CSTO members).

It is the geopolitical axis "Ankara-Baku-Tbilisi" that allowed, firstly, the AR to practically withdraw from the military-political influence of the Russian Federation (meaning the closure of the Gabala radar station), and secondly, official Baku, having secured Turkish and American support, is rigidly positioning itself to official Tehran.

At the same time, Turkey is currently not interested in a clash in the South Caucasus with the Russian Federation and the Islamic Republic of Iran (IRI). Moreover, the military and political situation around Syria and Iraq (including the Kurdish issue) has slowed down the progressive advancement of the foreign policy concept of official Ankara in the direction of the "East" (South Caucasus and Central Asia).

At present, Turkey, on the one hand, seeks to prevent the restoration of Russian positions in Georgia, and on the other hand, to strengthen its positions in the AR and Georgia, which minimizes the geopolitical significance of Russia's military and political presence in the RA. Although Turkey intends to oust the Russian Federation and IRI from the South Caucasus region in the medium term, objective conditions must mature in the region for this to happen.

In the context of the realization of Turkish aspirations with regard to the South Caucasus, official Ankara is interested in close economic cooperation with Georgia and the AR. Thus, Turkey is Georgia's largest trade partner. In addition, Turkey is also strengthening in Adjara.

In particular, most of the new buildings in Batumi were built by Turkish investors. Also, Turkish citizens have bought up many stores and other establishments in Batumi. According to various sources, the number of Turkish citizens permanently residing in the capital of Adjara has already reached 20 thousand people.

It can be assumed that after the Sochi Olympics in 2014 and the 100th anniversary of the so-called "Armenian genocide" in 1915, Turkey may go for dismantling the status quo in the South Caucasus region. The fact is that both the Armenian-Turkish and Armenian-Azerbaijani conflicts are on the same plane, which hinders the realization of the Turkish geopolitical project. Consequently, if the solution of the above-mentioned conflicts in a package option is not possible, the use of "soft power" in the Armenian-Azerbaijani conflict can form a regional negotiating platform: Turkey-AR-RA-Georgia, which meets the national and regional interests of official Ankara.

Presidents of the Republic of Azerbaijan (AR) and Turkey Ilham Aliyev and R. T. Erdogan discussed energy transport issues during bilateral talks in Baku on September 3, 2014, including such issues as the state and future of Azerbaijani-Armenian and Azerbaijani-Russian relations in the context of the results of the Sochi meeting of the Presidents of the AR, the Russian Federation (RF) and the Republic of Armenia on the political settlement of the Karabakh conflict; strengthening of military-technical cooperation (MTC) between the AR and Turkey in the context of the developments in the Balkan region; strengthening of the military-technical cooperation (MTC) between the AR and Turkey in the context of the Karabakh conflict resolution.

The hypothetical deployment of a Turkish military base on the territory of the Nakhchivan Autonomous Republic (NAR) is no longer a subject of discussion between the Presidents of Armenia and Turkey. The fact is that the deployment of foreign troops on the territory of the AR may lead to foreign policy pressure from the Russian Federation and the Islamic Republic of Iran (IRI) with all the ensuing negative consequences for official Baku. Therefore, it seems more realistic to establish an AR military base on the territory of the NAR, where Turkish military instructors will teach combat training and anti-terrorist struggle to servicemen of the Armed Forces (AF) and representatives of AR law enforcement agencies.

It can be assumed that official Baku and official Ankara will develop a joint strategy to create an effective regional security system in the South Caucasus region, taking into account the long-term national and regional interests of both Azerbaijan and Turkey, including the so-called "Armenian" issue.

Following the extraordinary parliamentary elections that took place on November 1, 2015, Turkey has become more active in the South Caucasus region to further strengthen its military, political and economic presence in the Republic of Azerbaijan and Georgia.

Regarding Armenia, Turkey solves its strategic goals and tactical tasks in the context of the resolution of the Karabakh conflict and the implementation of the Zurich Protocols. Although, official Ankara has a vested interest in the speedy resolution of the Azerbaijani-Armenian and Armenian-Turkish conflicts, as only in this case Turkey can, on the one hand, cover the entire South Caucasus region with its geopolitical and geo-economic influence, and on the other hand, neutralize the activity of the Islamic Republic of Iran in the countries of the region, as well as effectively control the actions of the Russian Federation in the South Caucasus.

Therefore, Turkey continues its efforts to institutionalize the Azerbaijani-Georgian-Turkish military-political alliance, which will allow official Ankara to transform itself into a major and effective geopolitical player, unlike the Russian Federation, the United States, the EU and the IRI. In addition, official Ankara is interested in the cooperation of Turkish law enforcement agencies with the countries of the Caucasus-Caspian region. Thus, in January 2013 in Baku, on Turkey's initiative, the "Eurasian Law Enforcement Association" was established with military status in Turkey, Azerbaijan, Kazakhstan and Kyrgyzstan. Symbolically, the Association was established with the aim of cooperation between Azerbaijan, Kazakhstan, Kyrgyzstan and Turkey in the issue of countering organized crime, terrorist and smuggling activities, activity of radical Islamist groups. It should be noted that the Islamic factor helps Turkey to promote its geopolitical, geo-economic and geo-cultural goals in the South Caucasus region. The fact is that the image of official Ankara is more attractive in comparison with Iran, since Turkey has a successful moderate Islam on the one hand and a secular political system combining elements of Western-style democracy on the other. The peculiarity of Turkey's foreign policy doctrine in the South Caucasus region is the following: official Ankara actively uses such tools as diplomacy and business structures, develops relations in bilateral and multilateral formats, and expands Turkic and Turkish cultural and political influence in Azerbaijan and Georgia.

In particular, Turkey's economic policy towards the countries of the South Caucasus is realized in the context of providing grants, loans and technical support. At the same time, Turkey does not associate itself in the South Caucasus region with the financing of major energy transportation and infrastructure projects (TANAP and TAP, Baku-Tbilisi-Ceyhan (BTC), Baku-Tbilisi-Kars (BTC), etc.).), but prefers to promote its commercial, cultural and educational programs, relying on non-state structures, but actively supported by official Ankara (the Turkish Cooperation and Development Agency (TIKA), the Organization for the Joint Development of Turkic Culture and Art

(TURKSOY), the Turkic Parliamentary Assembly, the Council of Elders and the Turkic Assembly under the Office of the Prime Minister of Turkey).

In this regard, it should be noted that Azerbaijan is considered a key state in Turkey's foreign policy in the South Caucasus region, as Azerbaijan is a Muslim country. By the way, one of the largest investors of Turkey is the SOCAR oil company. It is symbolic that Azerbaijan and Turkey signed a treaty "On Strategic Partnership and Mutual Assistance". The 10-year treaty stipulates that if one of the parties is attacked by a third country, both parties will provide mutual assistance to each other.

Other provisions of the Treaty oblige the parties to make joint efforts to eliminate threats to national security, to prohibit working with organizations that threaten the independence, sovereignty and territorial integrity of the other party, to prevent the use of their territories to commit acts of aggression against the other party, and to cooperate in the production of defense industry, joint military exercises and training of army specialists.

Turkey is developing mutually beneficial cooperation with Azerbaijan and Georgia, both within the framework of the Black Sea Economic Cooperation Organization (BSEC) as well as other international associations.

If Turkey and Azerbaijan are brought closer by the cultural and linguistic factor, ethnicity and religion (Islam), as well as participation in the Cooperation Council of Turkic Speaking States (CCTS), then in relations with Georgia, political issues, joint projects in the field of energy and transportation infrastructure are of greater importance for official Ankara. After all, Turkey is interested in Georgia as a country through whose territory it can safely transit cargoes to Russia and the Central Asian region (CAR) and further in the direction of the People's Republic of China (PRC).

Chapter 3: Prospects for Conflict Resolution in the South Caucasus

It can be stated that a political settlement of the Georgian-Abkhazian, Georgian-South Ossetian and Karabakh conflicts is not possible, as the resolution of the above conflicts within the territorial integrity of Azerbaijan and Georgia does not meet the Kremlin's regional interests in the Black Sea-Caucasus region.

First, both Azerbaijan and Georgia, for different reasons, are unwilling to participate in such economic and military-political integration projects in the post-Soviet space as the Customs Union (CU), the EAEU and the CSTO. In particular, while official Tbilisi makes no secret of its intentions to integrate into the EU and NATO structures, official Baku seeks to continue to successfully implement the policy of balance of power with both Russia and the West.

Secondly, official Moscow is trying to include Azerbaijan in the above-mentioned integration projects without giving official Baku real preferences and firm guarantees in the issues of restoration of the country's territorial integrity, as well as the Kremlin's non-interference in the internal and external affairs of the republic, and most importantly, in the process of decision-making and implementation (including in the issue of Azerbaijan's relations with the West and Turkey).

Thirdly, the Russian leadership is applying tactics of "soft pressure" on the part of Abkhazia and South Ossetia in relation to official Tbilisi. In particular, since 2008, about 40 meetings have been held within the framework of the Geneva Process for the political settlement of the Georgian-Abkhazian and Georgian-South Ossetian conflict, which have not yielded any practical results. For example, while official Tbilisi insists that the problem of territorial integrity of Georgia should be discussed in this format with the participation of international representatives of the U.S., EU, UN and OSCE, Abkhazia and South Ossetia demand from Georgia to recognize the independence of Abkhazia and South Ossetia and to sign an agreement on the non-use of force. But Georgia is ready to sign the above agreement only with the Russian Federation, but official Moscow says that the Russian Federation is not a party to the conflict and therefore refuses to sign an agreement with Georgia on non-use of force. It is symbolic that against this background Abkhazia and South Ossetia expressed their "concern about deepening Georgia's cooperation with NATO and the EU" immediately after the signing of the Association Agreement with the EU by official Tbilisi on June 27, 2014. And if we take into account that all statements by Abkhazian and South Ossetian officials are coordinated with the Kremlin, we can say that official Moscow will not change its position on the Georgian-Abkhazian and Georgian-South Ossetian conflicts with all the negative consequences that follow, both in the issue of the formation of an indivisible and effective security system in the South Caucasus region and the prospects for peaceful resolution of the two inter-ethnic conflicts.

Fourth, the Kremlin will continue its policy of manipulating the Georgian-Abkhazian and Georgian-South Ossetian conflicts within the framework of the Geneva negotiation process in order to curb Georgia's Euro-Atlantic integration.

Fifth, the main problem of the political elites of Azerbaijan and Georgia is the lack of creative approaches to resolving the Karabakh, Georgian-Abkhazian and Georgian-South Ossetian conflicts. Thus, the expectations of the leadership of Azerbaijan and Georgia are reduced to the possibility of replacing the Russian military-political presence in Armenia with the military-political presence of either the U.S., NATO or the EU in Armenia and Georgia, which will lead to the resolution of the above-mentioned conflicts. Although, this factor leads to the "unfreezing" of all conflicts in the South Caucasus region with all the ensuing negative consequences for Azerbaijan, Armenia and Georgia.

Conclusion: first, official Baku will continue its policy of non-participation or neutrality with regard to all integration processes in the post-Soviet space, as the political elites of Azerbaijan do not intend to delegate a part of its sovereignty to the executive bodies of the CU, EAEU and CSTO. It is logical that Azerbaijan is a member of the Movement of Non-Aligned Countries, which emphasizes the neutrality and equidistance of the republic from the CSTO and NATO.

Secondly, the U.S. seeks to seize the initiative from Russia within the OSCE Minsk Group, and on the other hand, to minimize the Kremlin's pressure on official Yerevan; to change the status quo in the negotiation process for the peaceful resolution of the Karabakh conflict by diplomatic means. The fact is that Washington takes as a real given the intention of official Baku to change the status quo in its favor, as Azerbaijan has all the necessary opportunities to do so.

It is logical that the ruling elites of Armenia also realize that, firstly, the possibility of resumption of hostilities in the ceasefire zone between the Armed Forces (AF) of both states remains, which is clearly evidenced by April 2016 with all the negative consequences that follow. The fact is that the election of Turkish President Rajab Tayyib Erdogan has further strengthened the negotiating position of I. Aliyev, as the head of the Turkish state publicly declared his support for official Baku. In addition, it was due to R.T. Erdogan's insistence that NATO's support for Azerbaijan's territorial integrity was stated in the final document of the Alliance summit. Moreover, official Ankara, represented by the Turkish President, promised its military-technical support in case official Baku decides to restore its territorial integrity through military force. It is true that official Yerevan is confident of Russia's military support in case of the outbreak of hostilities in the ceasefire zone. However, the isolation of official Moscow by the West due to the Ukrainian events minimizes the military and political possibilities of the Russian leadership in the South Caucasus region, including in the issue of providing military assistance to Armenia, as evidenced by the 4-day April war.

Thirdly, Russian initiatives within the framework of numerous meetings of the Presidents of the AR, RA and RF are more aimed at maintaining the status quo favorable to official Moscow and the aspiration of the Russian leadership to deploy its peacekeeping forces in the ceasefire zone between the Armed Forces of Azerbaijan and

Armenia, with all the consequences that this entails. In other words, official Moscow seeks to resolve the Karabakh conflict in the context of its regional interests, and it is natural that the current format of the OSCE Minsk Group fully satisfies the Russian leadership.

Therefore, the de facto composition of the OSCE MG may be enlarged by Turkey and the Islamic Republic of Iran, as well as the EU, with the active participation of the United States. In other words, Turkey, being a strategic ally of Azerbaijan, and IRI being an economic partner of Armenia in the South Caucasus region, will create the necessary balance of power and means for effective negotiation process and change of the status quo for the purpose of political solution of the Karabakh conflict.

Only in case of implementation of the above scenario, it is possible to achieve, firstly, neutralization of Russia and, as a consequence, change of the status quo in the interests of Azerbaijan and Armenia; secondly, minimization of the Kremlin's military-political and economic pressure on official Yerevan; thirdly, achievement of breakthrough results in the negotiation process on the resolution of the Karabakh conflict.

Conclusion: Azerbaijan's negotiating positions within the new configuration of the OSCE Minsk Group are superior to Armenia's. The fact is that official Yerevan, both in the negotiation process within the OSCE MG and in other dialog platforms (UN, CoE, PACE) is completely dependent on the Russian side. And if we take into account that official Tehran, represented by the President of the Islamic Republic of Iran Hussein Rouhani, demonstrates a more loyal policy towards Azerbaijan, then in the conditions of a serious crisis in the relations between the West and Russia, official Yerevan, following official Moscow, loses its room for maneuver.

Therefore, in light of a certain cooling of relations between Azerbaijan and the West, there is a tendency of intensive consultations between official Yerevan and the West (US, EU and NATO) on expanding and strengthening mutual cooperation.

In particular, despite the numerous military-political agreements concluded between

Armenia and Russia, official Yerevan speculates on the Kremlin's current negative image and turns it into a bargaining chip with the West. In other words, in the confrontation between the West and Russia, official Yerevan de facto supports the West for political and economic dividends. Moreover, the rapprochement between Armenia and the West will not allow official Yerevan to strengthen its position in the negotiation process for a political settlement of the Karabakh conflict.

The fact is that in official and expert circles of the West there is a point of view that the solution to the Karabakh conflict lies in the Euro-Atlantic integration of the South Caucasus countries. In other words, the Karabakh conflict will be positively resolved in favor of the state (either Azerbaijan or Armenia), where democratic values will be strong and which will take a course towards Euro-Atlantic integration. But, official Yerevan is not going to join the EU and NATO. Moreover, the above-mentioned structures do not see any real prerequisites for Armenia's Euro-Atlantic integration.

Conclusion: First, the U.S. seeks to form an anti-Russian coalition, including from the post-Soviet countries, in order to fight the Kremlin effectively and in the long term. All the more so as lower oil prices and the application of economic sanctions against Russia are beginning to yield serious results. Therefore, official Washington has not adopted sanctions against a number of Azerbaijani officials in the context of the so-called Magnitsky List.

Second, rapprochement between Azerbaijan and Russia with all its consequences is not possible today, as the official authorities of the republic fear the Kremlin's intention to involve the country in the EAEU. That is why after the unexpected visit of Russian Deputy Prime Minister Dmitry Rogozin to Baku in late December 2014 and his meeting with the President of Azerbaijan, the country's Foreign Minister Elmar Mammadyarov stated that the resolution of the Karabakh conflict is not a bargaining chip in the issue of the republic's entry into the EAEU and the CU.

Chapter 4. Relations between the South Caucasus states in bilateral and multilateral formats.

Relations between the South Caucasus states are built in a bilateral rather than multilateral format.

In particular, Azerbaijan, Armenia and Georgia have different approaches to regional security issues and are supported by opposing geopolitical actors. While Azerbaijan and Georgia are building long-term relationships with the US and the EU, Armenia is a member of the CSTO and the EAEU with all the consequences that entails.

In addition, the positions of Azerbaijan, Georgia and Armenia on the resolution of regional inter-ethnic conflicts differ. Azerbaijan and Georgia support the principle of territorial integrity (in the cases of Nagorno-Karabakh, Abkhazia and South Ossetia), while Armenia favors the principle of self-determination (Nagorno-Karabakh).

Moreover, due to the unresolved Karabakh conflict, official Baku does not accept the establishment of a multilateral model of regional cooperation in the South Caucasus region with the participation of official Yerevan.

And it can be assumed that in the medium term in the South Caucasus region, for objective reasons, the bilateral rather than multilateral format of relations between Azerbaijan, Armenia and Georgia will prevail. In other words, relations between the South Caucasus states will be built along the lines of Azerbaijan-Georgia and Georgia-Armenia.

At the same time, at present, the multilateral format of interstate relations in the South Caucasus region is possible only in the following configuration: Azerbaijan-Georgia-Turkey. Moreover, the multilateral format of Azerbaijan-Georgia-Turkey has both political and economic support from the U.S. and the EU (for example, the implementation of such energy transportation and infrastructure projects as the Baku-Tbilisi-Ceyhan (BTC) oil pipeline, the Baku-Tbilisi-Erzerum South Caucasus gas pipeline, the Baku-Tbilisi-Kars railway project, as well as the early implementation of TANAP and TAP became possible only thanks to the support of the U.S. and the EU).

It should also be noted that official Baku and official Ankara benefit from a political settlement of the Karabakh conflict. In particular, in this case, Turkey will achieve the resolution of the Armenian-Turkish conflict with all the ensuing positive consequences for the Turkish side, and the official authorities of Azerbaijan will diversify their energy transportation policy. After all, practically all energy transportation and infrastructure projects implemented by official Baku pass through Georgian territory with all the ensuing negative consequences for Azerbaijan.

The fact is that Tbilisi believes that the signed agreements between Azerbaijan, Georgia and Turkey should not have a negative impact on Armenian-Georgian relations, which does not meet the current national and regional interests of official Baku in the context of the Azerbaijani-Armenian confrontation.

In other words, official Tbilisi seeks to avoid a situation in which it has to choose between Azerbaijan and Armenia. Thus, within the ruling coalition in Georgia there is a group that considers it possible to open the Abkhazian railroad, which would actually take Armenia out of the transportation blockade and connect it with Russia. However, so far official Tbilisi has not taken practical steps to open the Abkhazian railroad, but it can be assumed that in case of warming of Georgian-Russian relations official authorities of Georgia may take an active part in restoration of the railroad "Armenia - Georgia - Russia". By the way, the Russian-Georgian checkpoint "Lars" has already provided a special "green corridor" for cargoes from Armenia to deliver goods from Armenia to Russia in an accelerated mode, which meets the national interests of official Yerevan in the context of the republic's accession to the EAEU.

In addition, during the land reform in Georgia, Azerbaijani families in the administrative-territorial region of Kvemo-Kartli (at least 400,000 Azerbaijanis live in Bolnisi, Marneuli and Gardabani) received only 15 hectares of land, while the average

Georgian family received 3-4 hectares under the same law. Moreover, there was a massive change of toponyms. Many Azerbaijani villages and settlements in Georgia were given Georgian names, which caused resentment not only among Georgian Azerbaijanis, but also in Azerbaijan.

Another serious incident occurred in 2011, when the Spiritual Administration of Muslims of the Caucasus (DUMK), headed by Sheikh Allahshukur Pashazadeh, did not support the establishment of the Spiritual Islamic Administration in Georgia, which began to exercise control over the activities of Muslim religious sites in the country.

In turn, Yerevan believes that Georgia is pushing Armenia out of regional politics and refuses to ratify the European Charter, which would give the Armenian language the status of a regional language on Georgian territory, including Javakheti. The fact is that the problem of Javakheti, an Armenian-populated region of Georgia, plays an important role in bilateral Armenian-Georgian relations. The fact that about 250,000 ethnic Armenians live in this administrative-territorial region bordering Armenia creates mutual suspicions and phobias.

Therefore, official Yerevan is closely following the cooperation of Azerbaijan, Georgia and Turkey, fearing the deepening of the existing transportation and communication blockade of Armenia by the above-mentioned three countries.

Although, the multilateral format of Azerbaijan-Georgia-Turkey is not a closed regional model of cooperation. Thus, back in 2008, at the height of the Georgian-Russian military confrontation, official Ankara stated that Azerbaijani-Georgian-Turkish interaction in the South Caucasus region is an open, not a closed format, and under certain conditions (if it corresponds to their interests) all interested parties can participate in it.

It is symbolic that during the August Georgian-Russian war R. T. Erdogan came up with an initiative to create a geopolitical association with the participation of the Caucasus countries (Azerbaijan, Georgia, Armenia and Russia), as well as the EU, the

US and Turkey - the "Caucasus Stability and Cooperation Platform".

By the way, Brussels also has a "Stability Pact for the Caucasus" developed by Michael Emerson in the following configuration: Azerbaijan, Georgia and Armenia + Russia, Turkey and the Islamic Republic of Iran + the US and the EU.

Official Ankara is not against Russia's participation in the multilateral regional format, as it is the Kremlin that has a real military-political resource of pressure on official Yerevan. But, on the one hand, official Moscow remained satisfied with the above position of Turkey, and on the other hand, refused to participate in the multilateral regional format of cooperation.

Chapter 5. The Nagorno-Karabakh conflict and the Armenian-Turkish protocols at the present stage

The Armenian Foreign Ministry believes that official Ankara should respect the agreements on ratification of protocols without preconditions. The Armenian Foreign Minister Edward Nalbandian has repeatedly stated this.

In E. Nalbandian's opinion, which he made on June 9, 2010 during the "government hour" in the Armenian Parliament, neither the Karabakh issue nor Armenian-Russian relations are under threat. According to the Minister, neither "NKR" nor Armenia intends to discuss the resolution of the Karabakh conflict in the Azerbaijani-Turkish format.

Commenting on the statements of official Baku that Armenia has not accepted the Madrid Principles to this day, the Minister reminded that Yerevan recognized this document as a basis for negotiations two years ago. In his opinion, the key issue in this document is the status of Nagorno-Karabakh. Commenting on the statements of the Azerbaijani side on the readiness to give Karabakh a high degree of autonomy within that state, the Minister noted that this is ignoring the provision on the expression of the will of the people. In addition, according to the Minister, official Baku also rejects the principle of non-use of force, unwilling to sign the document on the withdrawal of snipers from the line of contact.

According to the Armenian Foreign Ministry, official Yerevan adopted the Madrid Principles as a basis for negotiations more than two years ago. All other proposals of the mediators were of a working nature. Most importantly, Armenia's position on the updated Madrid principles for the settlement of the Nagorno-Karabakh conflict was expressed in St. Petersburg on June 17, 2010. In the opinion of Armenian experts, the trilateral meeting of the Presidents of Armenia, Russia and Azerbaijan held in St. Petersburg did not lead to anything. Azerbaijan excludes the possibility of full independence of Nagorno-Karabakh, while the Armenian side says "if you exclude this possibility, we will do nothing about the rest of the Madrid principles".

On June 24, 2010, Armenian President Sargsyan visited Stepanakert/Khankendi. The purpose of the visit was to familiarize the Karabakh leadership with the proposals made by the Russian side during the trilateral Sargsyan-Aliev-Medvedev meeting in St. Petersburg. We are talking about those "St. Petersburg proposals" that I. Aliyev allegedly approved in the presence of Medvedev and then rejected during the meeting with the OSCE Minsk Group Co-Chairs and returned to Baku. In fact, today there is a new document on the negotiating table, which the Armenian side allegedly agreed to accept as a basis for continuing negotiations on the basic Madrid principles.

According to former U.S. Ambassador to Armenia Marie Yovanovitch, Armenians and Turks have more uniting than dividing factors. The U.S. supports the continuation of the process of establishing relations between Armenia and Turkey. According to her, the opening of borders is beneficial for all, and first of all for the parties themselves. It is important for the U.S. that Armenia be more developed and its economy be more stable, as in that case Washington will have a stronger and more reliable partner in the person of Yerevan. The former Ambassador cited research data, according to which, if the Armenian-Turkish border is opened, the Armenian economy will have 3% growth annually. Ms. Yovanovitch welcomed the recent statement of the Armenian President, which, according to her, shows that Armenia has not given up negotiations with Turkey and is ready to resume them as soon as official Ankara is ready for it. In M. Jovanovic's opinion, the fact that Turkey has started to talk and discuss complex historical issues can be considered a great progress. She admitted that the process of normalization of relations is not developing as fast as expected, but there is some progress.

Armenian President Serzh Sargsyan said at a meeting with representatives of the Armenian community in Rostov-on-Don that Armenia does not intend to bargain over the Karabakh issue around the right of the people of Karabakh to self-determination. In his opinion, Turkey's unwillingness to ratify the Armenian-Turkish protocols was the main reason for the freezing of the process on the part of official Yerevan. Moreover, Turkey is trying to interfere in the Karabakh settlement process, where it has nothing to do, the Armenian President emphasized.

Vahan Hovhannisyan, head of the parliamentary faction of the Armenian Revolutionary Federation "Dashnaktsutyun" (ARF), believes that the country's leadership is obliged, first, to withdraw the signatures under the Armenian-Turkish protocols and stop talking about the readiness to continue the dialog without preconditions. Secondly, not to allow changing the negotiation format for the settlement of the Karabakh conflict. According to V. Hovhannisyan, the European Parliament resolution on the South Caucasus contains one more dangerous provision than the paragraphs contained in the section on Nagorno Karabakh. He noted that in the section "European Strategy" it is mentioned about replacing the French co-chairmanship in the OSCE Minsk Group with the EU co-chairmanship. The MP explained that perhaps first the representative of France will be given the mandate of the EU, and then the issue of rotation will arise. This may lead to the proposal to give the representative of Russia the CIS mandate in the future. In V. Hovhannisyan's opinion, the danger of such an initiative is that different EU member states have different positions on the settlement of the Karabakh conflict. According to V. Hovhannisyan, not only Azerbaijan questions the mandate of the OSCE Minsk Group, but also the European Parliament itself. Therefore, the deputy believes that the goal of the Armenian authorities should be to prevent this process.

The U.S., as co-chair of the OSCE Minsk Group, sees the possibility of progress, but the most difficult question is what happens after Armenia and Azerbaijan accept the basic principles for resolving the Karabakh conflict. The issue must be resolved solely on the basis of compromise, and political will is needed to achieve lasting peace.

In particular, the Armenian Parliament's Committee on Foreign Relations, at its June 3, 2010 session, gave a negative opinion on the draft law "On Recognition of the

'Nagorno-Karabakh Republic'" initiated by representatives of the Heritage faction. The Secretary of the faction Larisa Alaverdyan noted that taking into account the recently adopted European Parliament resolution on the South Caucasus, Armenia should take appropriate steps, one of which could be the inclusion of the draft law in the parliament's big agenda. Earlier, the Armenian government gave a negative conclusion to the draft law "On Recognition of the Nagorno-Karabakh Republic" at the session of November 12, 2009. Armenia's Deputy Foreign Minister Shavarsh Kocharyan stated on behalf of the executive body that the adoption of such a law was inexpedient at this stage.

According to Armenian experts, the danger of resumption of hostilities in Nagorno-Karabakh has increased extremely at the moment. In their opinion, the threat is posed by a radical change in the position of the Islamic Republic of Iran on the Karabakh issue. The fact that the IRI is now in favor of changing the military-political status quo speaks about the existence of a real threat in the South Caucasus region. Especially since the IRI came forward with an initiative to become a mediator on the Karabakh settlement. While Azerbaijan immediately accepted official Tehran's proposal, Armenia decided to remain silent. Armenian experts believe that the Turkish-Azerbaijani tandem gave certain guarantees to IRI that if the latter joins them and takes a similar position on Karabakh, peacekeeping forces will not enter the region. The Armenian president's statement in Brussels is defined by experts as a warning signal to official Tehran about the danger of NATO troops appearing near its borders in case the existing status quo is changed. On the other hand, Sargsyan's statement in Brussels turned out to be the first veiled appeal for help to NATO in the post-Soviet space after the Russian-Georgian war in August 2008. Moreover, this appeal came not from Georgian President Mikheil Saakashvili, but from the president of Armenia, a country that is a member of the CSTO, i.e. Russia's military ally. And this is a message to the Kremlin.

In turn, official Tehran adheres to the view that conflict and confrontation cannot have a positive impact on the development of countries, and IRI's position on the Karabakh conflict remains the same - there can be no alternative to a peaceful resolution of the problem. As for the initiative of official Tehran to act as an intermediary country in the conflict settlement process, taking into account the good neighborly relations with all countries of the region, IRI could play an important role in this issue. However, whether any changes should be made to the OSCE Minsk Group format should be decided by the negotiating parties themselves, the Iranian side believes.

The Turkish leadership suspended the Zurich process on the political settlement of Armenian-Turkish relations, linking the ratification of the signed protocols to the liberation of the occupied regions around Nagorno-Karabakh.

In other words, Turkey, despite US and EU pressure, supported official Baku, which opposed a differentiated approach to the process of normalization of Armenian-Turkish relations and the political settlement of the Karabakh conflict.

In the context of resolving the Karabakh conflict, official Yerevan has recently sought, on the one hand, to achieve the return of the "NKR" ("Republic of Artsakh") to the negotiation process under the auspices of the OSCE Minsk Group, thus transferring to Stepanakert/Khankendi the right to negotiate with official Baku with all the ensuing consequences, and, on the other hand, to split the Azerbaijani-Turkish tandem.

It was the rigid position of official Baku that hindered the political settlement of the Armenian-Turkish conflict, which de facto led to the linkage in the resolution of the two conflicts with all the ensuing consequences.

It is symbolic that the need to return "NKR" to the negotiation process on the political settlement of the Karabakh conflict within the framework of the OSCE MG is periodically stated not only by the official authorities of Aomenia, but also by some official representatives of Russia, the USA and France (co-chairs of the OSCE MG). At the same time, in the issue of determining the status of "NKR" through the liberation of the occupied Azerbaijani territories around "NKR" (except for Lachin corridor and

Kelbajar district) Yerevan refers to the priority right of Karabakh Armenians to determine their fate, which implies either independent status of "NKR" or incorporation into Armenia, but not even formal stay within Azerbaijan.

Therefore, the compromise of official Baku announced by the AR Foreign Minister E. Mammadyarov is "territories in exchange for peace". The fact is that official Baku does not want to consider "NKR" as a party to the Karabakh conflict. It is obvious that Armenia and "NKR", having secured the support of the Armenian Diaspora in France, the United States and Russia, as well as the official authorities of these countries due to different geopolitical interests, will not accept the above-mentioned compromise of the Azerbaijani side. Especially since the hypothetical implementation of the "territory for peace" model neutralizes all the advantages and opportunities of the Armenian side in terms of ensuring the security of "NKR", and as a consequence, leads to the full control of official Baku over "NKR".

In other words, the hypothetical realization of the "territory for peace" model within the framework of the negotiation process under the auspices of the OSCE MG or the refusal of the official Armenian authorities from the Azerbaijani plan of peaceful resolution of the Karabakh conflict leads to a direct military confrontation between Azerbaijan and Armenia, but with one important condition: the next Azerbaijani-Armenian war can start from the military-political positions more convenient for official Baku.

It is logical that official Baku seeks to liberate the territories along the Arax River, which from the east close in on Armenia's Meghri district. It is this direction of the main strike of the Azerbaijani Armed Forces that was one of the main ones during the 4-day April war. In addition, official Baku together with Turkey is building up and strengthening the military grouping in the Nakhchivan Autonomous Republic (NAR), already from the west of Meghri.

It can be stated that the above-mentioned and other actions of the Azerbaijani-Turkish tandem can be regarded as coercion of official Yerevan to the Azerbaijani plan.

Therefore, official Yerevan seeks to split the Azerbaijani-Turkish tandem, which is not possible. Yerevan believes that this is possible if official Yerevan gets closer to the EU and the U.S. against the backdrop of cooling relations between the West and Turkey. Although, official Ankara may distance itself from a solution to the Karabakh conflict within the framework of the Azerbaijani plan only in case of a real threat of the creation of a Kurdish state, which would require the Kremlin's help to prevent.

At the same time, official Moscow, on the one hand, is still able to prevent the military scenario of the situation in the Karabakh conflict zone, and on the other hand, to preserve the current status quo for the resolution of the Karabakh conflict in the distant future.

Therefore, it can be stated that at present the development of the situation in the Karabakh conflict zone will not lead to full-scale hostilities between the Azerbaijani and Armenian Armed Forces.

And the latest statements of AR President Ilham Aliyev indicate that official Baku will seek international isolation of Armenia, which should force official Yerevan to sit down at the negotiating table under the auspices of the OSCE Minsk Group on Azerbaijani terms. It can be assumed that this strategy of official Baku is not realizable, as both Russia and the West will not go for the isolation of Armenia, let alone the adoption of sanctions against official Yerevan.

Chapter 6. On tendencies of Islamization of the regions of Georgia and Armenia, confrontation between Sunnis and Shiites in Azerbaijan

At present, unlike Georgia, there is no obvious trend of Islamization in Armenia due to the mono-ethnic composition of the country's population (mainly ethnic Armenians) and, as a consequence, the dominance of the Armenian Apostolic Church throughout the country. In addition, the official authorities of Armenia pursue a policy of preserving one religion in the republic - Christianity.

Although, Armenians who have converted to Islam - Amshen Armenians (about 800 thousand), live in the North Caucasus of Russia, Turkey, Georgia and CAR. It is symbolic that about 200 families of Amshen Armenian Muslims from the Kyrgyz Republic (KR), ready to resettle in Azerbaijani lands occupied by Armenia, have never received an invitation from official Yerevan.

However, many Armenians leaving Armenia due to economic hardship go to Turkey and other Arab countries where they embrace Islam. As a rule, these are Armenian women who marry locals.

At the same time, the number of Shiite Iranians, among whom there are many ethnic Azeris from South Azerbaijan of the Islamic Republic of Iran, has been growing in Armenia in recent years. Thus, Iranians, moving with their whole families, buy real estate and open businesses in Armenia. By the way, there is a Shiite mosque with a cultural center in Yerevan, Iranian banks, as well as restaurants with national cuisine.

As for the trend of Islamization of Georgia's regions, the aforementioned trend is taking place mainly in Adjara, where Turkey's positions are getting stronger every year.

Currently, all major hotels, casinos, restaurants, bars, as well as the airport in Adjara belong to Turkish businessmen. And that is why Turkish neighborhoods have appeared in Adjara. According to various estimates, more than 8 thousand Sunni Turks live in Batumi today.

In recent years, several Islamic educational institutions have been opened in Adjara, which are unable to accommodate all those who wish to attend.

Although, the current official authorities of Georgia, unlike ex-president Mikheil Saakashvili, have suspended the process of granting Georgian citizenship to natives of Turkey, as well as Meskhetian Turks (according to various sources, more than 100 thousand people).

By the way, the work of all public organizations of Meskhetian Turks is supported to a greater or lesser extent by the Government and Parliament of Turkey.

In turn, M. Saakashvili granted Georgian citizenship to more than 2 thousand Turkish citizens of Georgian origin who profess Sunni Islam. In addition, during Saakashvili's time Georgian authorities granted citizenship to 25 thousand Turks living in Adjara (these citizens have dual citizenship). Moreover, under M. Saakashvili a law was adopted obliging official Tbilisi to resettle Meskhetian Turks in Javakheti, where about 250 thousand Georgian Armenians live. Symbolically, the provisions of the above-mentioned law have not been fulfilled by the official Georgian authorities to this day.

In Azerbaijan, against the background of the weakening of Shiite religious communities and, as a consequence, a decrease in the number of followers of Shiite Islam, there is a process of some strengthening of the positions of Wahhabi jamaats.

The fact is that Wahhabis consider both Shiites and Sunnis to be heretics (the well-known events in Syria and Iraq are clear evidence of this). According to the Wahhabis, only they are "muwahhidun" Muslims (monotheists).

It should also be noted that domestic Wahhabis do not recognize the existing Sunni madhhabs. In other words, the Wahhabis consider themselves adherents of the trans-Mazhab ideology, which refers to the early or "correct" Islam.

It is symbolic that the 4th mandatory re-registration of all religious organizations in Azerbaijan has taken place since 1991. As a result of the above re-registration, radical Wahhabi jamaats were excluded from the register of legal entities. In addition, the law enforcement agencies of Azerbaijan periodically neutralize small armed groups of Wahhabis in the northern regions of the country.

31

Chapter 7: Trends in economic development, possible destabilization of the situation in the countries of the South Caucasus

Intensification of Georgian-NATO relations may lead to aggravation of the military-political situation around Georgia with all the ensuing negative consequences for Azerbaijan and Armenia.

In particular, in the short term, Azerbaijan is not threatened by financial and budgetary crisis. Thus, the gold and foreign exchange reserves of the AR amount to more than 4.825 billion dollars, and the reserves of the State Oil Fund of Azerbaijan (SOFAZ) are estimated at about 40 billion dollars.

It should be noted that the government of Azerbaijan is working on building a new model of economic development of the country, which will be able to protect the republic from negative influences from outside. In particular, the new model of Azerbaijan's economic development is based on the diversification of the economy of the republic, i.e. the government emphasizes its efforts on the development of domestic production, including industrial, agricultural sector, tourism, ICT, as well as actively invests in education in order to build a "knowledge economy". And in case of realization of the above model, the government will achieve sustainable growth of Azerbaijan's economy for the long-term period.

In the Georgian economic sphere, the trend is to strengthen the bilateral U.S.-Georgian investment protection treaty, which is designed to increase official Tbilisi's access to the Generalized System of Preferences, as well as to create conditions for a free trade agreement between Georgia and the United States.

In addition, official Tbilisi seeks to solve the problem of energy security, which involves increasing Georgia's energy production, improving energy efficiency, as well as strengthening the physical security of energy transit through Georgian territory towards the EU.

As for the pro-Western rhetoric of official Tbilisi, according to authoritative Georgian experts, the official authorities are trying to use it to strengthen Georgia's position in the negotiation process within the framework of the Geneva process.

At the same time, official Washington's intention to deploy a NATO base and missile defense system in Georgia in the short term is fraught with destabilization of the socio-political situation in the country, as well as aggravation of the Georgian-South Ossetian and Georgian-Abkhazian conflicts with all the negative consequences that follow.

And it can be stated that the United States initiated this process. In particular, in August 2015, a NATO training center was established in Georgia, which combined several training and tactical areas - the Krtsanisi National Training Center in Tbilisi and the facilities of the Vaziani military base, including a tactical field and firing range. Symbolically, the Center is designed for joint training of military personnel from NATO countries, partner countries and the Georgian military.

In its turn, Armenia has joined the EAEU, which will determine the tendencies of the republic's economic development. According to Armenian experts, Armenia's membership in the EAEU can minimize the negative consequences of the economic crisis in the country.

It should be noted that Armenia and the Islamic Republic of Iran intend to initiate negotiations on the establishment of a free trade zone (FTA). The initiative belongs to official Tehran.

It can be assumed that after the lifting of the tough economic sanctions of the UN Security Council, the EU and the US against the IRI, the possible establishment of an FTA between the RA and the IRI will not contradict official Yerevan's obligations to the CU and the EAEU. Thus, Iranian goods coming from the territory of the Republic of Armenia to the CU zone will be subject to the appropriate duty.

However, the idea of building the "IRI - RA" railroad lobbied by official Yerevan will completely lose its significance after the "Kazvin - Resht - Astara" railroad is put into operation.

"Qazvin - Resht - Astara" will connect the Iranian railroad system with the Azerbaijani one, and the IRI will have an opportunity to access in the direction of Russian and Georgian seaports.

In other words, after the commissioning of the Kazvin-Resht-Astara railroad, the Iranian side will not need a railroad branch to Armenia for purely economic reasons. Especially since official Tbilisi opposes the reanimation of the Abkhazian railroad, which is in the interests of the "North-South" and "Baku-Tbilisi-Kars" transport corridor.

The internal political situation in Azerbaijan and Armenia is stable, and currently there are no subjective reasons and conditions for destabilization of the socio-political and socio-economic situation in both countries.

In addition, despite the military rhetoric in Baku and Yerevan, thanks to the efforts of the Russian side, the Karabakh conflict is under strict control, which does not allow either side of the conflict to break or change the status quo in its favor.

With regard to Georgia and the Georgian-Abkhazian and Georgian-South Ossetian inter-ethnic military conflicts, there is currently a deteriorating dynamic in the military and political situation in and around Georgia.

In particular, the parties in Geneva are unsuccessfully discussing the issue of signing an agreement on the non-use of force, which the representatives of Abkhazia and South Ossetia have been trying to put on the agenda for 7 years with the support of Russia.

But official Tbilisi refuses to sign such an agreement, believing that Abkhazia and South Ossetia are not independent parties to the conflict. In turn, the official Georgian authorities demand that Russia commit to not using force against Georgia, to which official Moscow says it does not recognize itself as a party to the conflict and therefore refuses to sign the agreement.

In other words, the Geneva talks are doomed to failure, as the Georgian side is not willing to sign the above agreement, which de facto and de jure recognizes Abkhazia and South Ossetia as parties to the conflict.

However, this circumstance will not stop the integration of Abkhazia and South Ossetia with Russia. Especially since in December 2014 and March 2015 Russia and Abkhazia and South Ossetia signed agreements "On Union and Integration". In contrast to the Abkhaz-Russian announcement, the Russian-South Ossetian agreement implies even greater integration of South Ossetia with Russia, with all the resulting negative consequences for Georgia. The fact is that the official Georgian authorities refuse to meet with the Russian leadership.

It can be assumed that the pro-Western foreign policy course of the official Georgian authorities is fraught with aggravation of the internal political situation for official Tbilisi, both in the country and in relations with Abkhazia and South Ossetia.

Symbolically, the positions of pro-Russian political forces are strengthening in Georgia, and the number of supporters of improving relations with Russia is growing, which is in the Kremlin's regional interests.

Thus, according to a survey conducted in Georgia by the American non-governmental organization (NGO) represented by the National Democratic Institute (N01), although support for Georgia's Euro-Atlantic course among the population still prevails, there is some growth in the number of those who would like to see the country in the EAEU.

Chapter 8: On the development of the socio-political situation in the South Caucasus region (conclusions)

Conclusions: First, the Georgian authorities will continue their policy of cooperation with the West in the short term, both in military-technical cooperation (MTC), political and economic. It is logical that the U.S. military assistance program is focused on strengthening Georgia's defense capabilities and deepening its compatibility with the U.S. and NATO. But most importantly, the program is aimed at preparing Georgia for the day when NATO decides to admit official Tbilisi to the Alliance. In this case, Azerbaijan's Euro-Atlantic integration will become real, with all its consequences.

At the same time, official Brussels did not provide Georgia with a Membership Action Plan (MAP) at the NATO summit held in Warsaw in July 2016. The fact is that there is no consensus in NATO on the issue of granting Georgia a MAP, as Germany and France fear a negative reaction from the Russian Federation. Official Moscow has repeatedly stated that it will not allow NATO expansion to the east, that "it will have catastrophic consequences".

Secondly, it is obvious that official Moscow, against the background of Russia's involvement in the well-known events in Syria and Ukraine, as well as the deterioration of macro- and microeconomic indicators of the Russian economy due to Western sanctions, has minimized its activity both in relation to Georgia and in the South Caucasus region as a whole. However, the Kremlin will continue to exert political pressure on the Georgian authorities through the international Geneva talks on stability and security in the Caucasus. Symbolically, the Russian Foreign Ministry's statement in connection with the 35th round of the international Geneva talks on stability and security in the Caucasus, which took place on March 22-23, 2016, expressed dissatisfaction with the deepening cooperation between Georgia and NATO. In addition, official Moscow condemned Georgia for refusing to sign a joint statement on the non-use of force "as a first step towards legally binding agreements between

Abkhazia, Georgia and South Ossetia." **Thirdly, the** Kremlin, exerting military and political pressure on Georgia, indirectly pressurizes official Baku as well. Therefore, the official authorities of Azerbaijan together with Turkey and Georgia intend to deepen military-political cooperation between the three countries.

However, official Baku, despite its strategic relationship with Turkey, continues to maintain partnership relations with Russia. Baku realizes that a political settlement of the Karabakh conflict is impossible without the Kremlin. Although, in case the current status quo is maintained in the Karabakh conflict zone, the official authorities of Azerbaijan will intensify their relations with Turkey and the West, which is what is happening today. True, there are no Turkish military bases on the territory of Azerbaijan yet (which cannot be ruled out in the future), but the level of military-trade relations between Azerbaijan and Turkey is growing to a full-fledged military-political alliance.

The high level of Azerbaijani-Turkish-Georgian relations allows the three countries, together with the EU, to successfully participate in the realization of the Southern Gas Corridor project, including the construction of the TANAP gas pipeline and the TAP gas branch.

After all, the main purpose of building these projects is considered to be to increase the security of natural gas supplies to Europe and potentially eliminate Russia as a monopoly in the role of supplier. The EU also aims to create alternative transportation routes for natural gas from CAR and the South Caucasus, bypassing Ukraine, which is de facto at war with Russia.

Fourth, since late 2016, Azerbaijan, Georgia and Turkey have started full operation of the almost completed Baku-Tbilisi-Kars (BTC) highway, which could become an element of the Silk Road. In combination with the Iranian-Azerbaijani railroad within the framework of the "North-South" project, the BTC completely nullifies the "Armenian project" and, consequently, makes the railroad blockade of Armenia, which has lasted for more than 20 years, almost complete, and, most importantly, prolongs it until the Karabakh conflict is resolved.

In addition, BTC and "North-South" neutralize Armenia's attempts to deblock the "Abkhazian Railway" (AJD), which is also losing its role as an important transit link capable of connecting the Islamic Republic of Iran and Armenia with Russia and other EAEU member states.

Fifth, the official Armenian authorities are returning to their traditional foreign policy doctrine: "both Russia and the West". The fact is that Yerevan believes that Armenia did not receive the expected dividends from joining the EAEU in January 2015 (except for the low price of natural gas). Thus, the economic crisis in Russia and the collapse of the ruble have directly affected the Armenian economy: transfers from Russia have sharply decreased, Armenian guest workers are returning to the republic from Russia, and exports of goods from Armenia to Russia have decreased. By the way, high-ranking Armenian officials have repeatedly emphasized that Armenia's accession to the CU is not part of their plans. As for the Russian claim that Armenia's accession to the EAEU solves security issues as well, it is illogical, as they are stipulated within the framework of the Armenian-Russian bilateral treaty.

Therefore, official Yerevan resumed negotiations with the EU on a new document regulating the relations between the parties. It should be noted that official Yerevan demonstrates readiness to sign the document. This was evidenced by the visit of the EU High Representative for Foreign Affairs and Security Policy Federica Mogherini to Yerevan on March 1, 2016.

By the way, after the meeting with F. Mogherini, RA Foreign Minister Eduard Nalbandian confirmed that Yerevan is ready to cooperate with the EU in all directions, but reminded that it will be done taking into account "other integration projects" referring to the country's participation in the EAEU.

List of references used

1. A. Hasanov "National Development and Security Policy of the Republic of Azerbaijan". Baku 2014. 670 c.

2. C. Veliyev, R. Resullu, K. Aslanli "Azerbaycan-Turkiye: dostluq, karde^lik ve strateji ortalik derleyenler", Ankara, 2012. 219 s.

3. Armenian-Azerbaijani conflict: history, law, mediation / I.M.Mammadov, T.F.Musayev. Baku 2008 (2nd edition, revised and supplemented) - 196 p.

4. O. Kuznetsov, "The Truth about the "Myths" of the Karabakh Conflict", Moscow: Minushchestvo 2013. 216 c.

5. V. Qasimli, Z. Şiriyev, Z. Voliyeva "iran-Ermonistan munasibotlori: geosiyasi realliq siyasi iddialar". B. 2011. 45 s.

6. A. V. Glazova "Turkey's Foreign Policy Initiatives in the South Caucasus: Success or Failure? Problems of National Strategy No. 1 (6) 2011.

7. Thomas de Waal, "The Karabakh Trap: Threats and Dilemmas of the Nagorno-Karabakh Conflict", Conciliation Resources, London, United Kingdom. 17 p.

8. Y. Kogan, "South Caucasus Countries and Security Issues," Neighborhood Policy Series, March 2013, The Black Sea Trust for Regional Cooperation, The German Marshall Fund of the United States, Bucharest, Romania. 9 c.

9. A. A. Sotnichenko Turkey: the geopolitical axis of Eurasia // Geopolitics. Vol. IX. M., 2011. C. 6.

10. Д. Eyvazov "Security of the Caucasus and Stability of Development of the Republic of Azerbaijan", Baku 2004, 358 p.

Printed by Books on Demand GmbH, Norderstedt / Germany